MORE THAN A THRESHOLD

More Than a Threshold

HEATHER SANDERSON

Published in North America by Majestic Wisdom Publishing.
Brooklyn, NY, USA
Georgetown, ON, Canada

www.majesticwisdompublishing.com

ISBN: 978-1-997539-19-3

Edited by Talaya Delaney
Cover art by Adobe Stock Images
Layout and Design by Heather Sanderson

CONTENTS

~ 1 ~

CRITICAL ESSAY:
INTRODUCTION

B e it a wardrobe, a rabbit hole, a mirror, train platform 9 and ¾, a hedgerow, a drawing on a sidewalk or a painting, a cave, a book, a ring, a door at the end of a hallway, a story within a story, or countless other examples, portals are a common literary device. A portal often exists in a story to provide a clear entry point for a character to physically leave one world (often the human world) and enter another. The use of a portal tells the reader to suspend the reality of everyday life and that it is okay to accept and believe the unknown possibilities of a fictional place; its presence and use give the reader permission to imagine. Portals, however, are more than a gateway to a reader's imagination and a threshold from one world to another. The specific kind of portal in a story functions as an integral and interconnected component of character transformation and gives the reader clues about exactly what kind of transformation to expect. To show this, I'll explore three texts that each have a very different kind of portal: *The Neverending Story* by Michael Ende, *She Never Told Me About the Ocean* by Elisabeth Sharp McKetta, and "Bluebeard's Egg" by Margaret Atwood.

That I've chosen three texts where the portal is so different (a book in *The Neverending Story*, a cave to the Underworld in *She Never Told Me About the Ocean*, and an imaginary egg in a story within a story in "Bluebeard's Egg") is important and intentional. It allows me to look at what is common in all three of these texts (a portal) and share why various kinds of choices and treatments are necessary depending on the kind of story and character transformation you want to write. In particular I'll look across these texts to discuss how and why to choose a portal "on purpose," what activates the portal or what the key is, and how to integrate the character's transformation with the portal by focusing on and developing the relationship between them.

~ 2 ~

WHAT IS A PORTAL?

If a portal is more than a threshold, then a working definition of what they are is helpful for the purposes of this paper. My own definition of a portal hinges on that of Lori Campbell. In *Portals of Power*, Campbell states that "by drawing our gaze to exact places where consciousness and un-consciousness meet, the portal spotlights the intricate human processes by which we navigate the world, ourselves, and the relationship between the two" and that a portal functions "to initiate a process of transformation on numerous levels—social, psychological, political, and spiritual" and "as a magical agent of transformation, the portal creates a way out, or a removal from the mundane, but its main function is as a way in, or inward" (Campbell 2, 6, 10). A portal, then, in literary fiction is an object (either physical or not) or a place that, by virtue of a character being in relationship with it, gives both the character and the reader first-hand and immediate access to their inner world. Why is this important or useful to keep in mind as writer?

To me, this means that character transformation is the very nature of story. As W.H. Auden points out in his essay "The Quest Hero," "human 'nature' is a nature continually in quest of itself, obliged every moment to transcend what it was a moment before" (81). All of life, then is a quest, and our human-made stories reflect that reality of life in countless iterations. When it comes to fiction writing and the modern story (be it a novel or otherwise) we tell and read stories for much of the same reason: to discover something about human nature. Be it our own or someone else's. This is an endless process, and we are constant learners who look both inside ourselves and outside of ourselves for this knowledge. It stands to reason that a character would do the same and that we, as readers, look to characters for this information. As a character transforms over the course of a story, a portal is not only a helpful anchor to keep the reader oriented in place and action, it also provides a reason for the character to reveal something about themselves and their situation. Yet again, why is this important?

In her discussion of characterization, in *Writing Fiction: A Guide to Narrative Craft*, Janet Burroway says, "for the most part, people in books encounter new situations and must work mentally towards understanding them; or they encounter old situations and must think them through anew" (79). This might seem simple, but in terms of defining character transformation, it's very helpful, especially in relation to when Burroway states that "every story is a pattern of change (events connected, as the author E.M. Forster observed, primarily by cause and effect) in which small and large changes are made through decision and discovery" (69). Every story, then, includes a character who must deal with at least one situation in their life and, through the decisions they make and the actions they take, they (either knowingly or unknowingly) change in some way from the beginning of the story to the end. Every story does not include a portal.

Why, then should a writer consider including a portal in their work? What does it achieve? And how can it be done in such a way that the portal is so engrained in the story that it does not feel like a prop to merely move the story forward, but as a necessary and inextricable component of the narrative? To answer these questions, I will look at three different kinds of portals in three works: the physical artefact of the storybook in *The Neverending Story* by Michael Ende, the cave to the Underworld in *She Never Told Me About the Ocean* by Elisabeth Sharp McKetta, and the intangible egg (as it exists only as an element of a story told orally to the protagonist, Sally by her Narrative Literature teacher) in "Bluebeard's Egg," by Margaret Atwood. It's important to show three completely different kinds of portals and how they work to tell different kinds of transformation stories so that a writer can think critically about what kind of a portal to implement in their work.

To better understand how to craft a portal I will also share three main aspects to consider when including one in a piece of fiction. They are:

1. Choose a Portal that is on Purpose: The kind of portal you choose equates to the kind of transformation (or failed transformation) you want a character to experience and, within that, how the protagonist discovers the portal matters as it is also a clue to the reader for what to expect.

2. There Needs to be a Key to the Portal: What is the mechanism to show that the worlds are merging? Often this key is an action the character needs to take, or they need to have special knowledge to gain access.

3. The Constraint of Relationship is Necessary: To not have a portal feel like a prop, the character is put "in conversation" with the portal. In other words, the two must be in a relationship and how they relate to one another drives the plot of character transformation. This constraint of relationship also leads the writer to make new discoveries they may not have had about the character without this relationship, which allows the story to go where it needs to go.

~ 3 ~

CHOOSE A PORTAL THAT IS
ON PURPOSE

The kind of portal in a story reflects the kind of story that is being told and the kind of transformation the character will undergo. To this end, the nature or character of the portal itself must be carefully considered. In other words, it doesn't just have to be there on purpose as in selected appropriately, or a good fit, but as if it is living out its life's purpose on the page just as the character is doing to communicate their story to the reader. To illustrate this, I'll provide a synopsis of *The Neverending Story*, *She Never Told Me About the Ocean*, "Bluebeard's Egg," and show how the nature of the portal in each reflects the kind of transformation that takes place.

In *The Neverending Story* Bastian Balthazar Bux is a "fat little boy of ten or twelve" who is grieving the loss of his mother (Ende 5). He runs into Carl Conrad Coreander's Old Books to escape from "the others"—children who are bullying him at school—and steals a book also called *The Neverending Story* which he then proceeds to read. Bastian knows that this book had "called to him in some mysterious way," and brought him into the shop to begin with, he is unaware (as is the reader) that the book is a portal to another world called Fantastica (Ende 11). Bastian enters Fantastica as a savior of the land. As he becomes power-hungry and loses touch with who he really is, his insecurities transform him into a dictator. He then begins to lose the last memories of himself and almost gets stuck in Fantastica forever. In the end, he recovers himself and learns how to be a loving person with courage and integrity that he brings back with him when he returns to his world. He returns, transformed, and his inner world would not have changed from that of an insecure child to a person with integrity without his journey with the portal of the book. The journey in this case is the anecdote to Bastian's initial condition—he becomes who he needs to be, yet he does not set out with a specific intention (at all) to seek transformation or change at the beginning of the novel.

The book as portal reflects the nature of his transformation because, once one is no longer a child and, unless there are reasons or desires otherwise, is rarely read to by someone else anymore, reading a book and learning from it is a solitary endeavor. The choice of a book as portal then mirrors the fact that Bastian's transformation is one that only he can do. The nature of the portal is aligned with the purpose of the journey: this is a one-way-one-person linear story. Just like a book is turned one page and then the next. And it is up to Bastian to make each decision along the way (just as the reader decides to keep reading). Yes, there are helper characters along the way, but his inner transformation is solely his and up to him.

In crafting a portal, the writer should carefully choose how the character discovers the portal as this is also an indicator of the type of transformation that might occur. If the character finds the portal on their own and by "accident," and it's an artefact, then it indicates that they are unaware of the desire for inner/psychological transformation but need it. Bastian isn't seeking personal transformation outright at the beginning of the story. He doesn't have to go into the bookshop and find the book, but if he did not then he would stay stuck in a pattern of being bullied and feeling like an outsider. He decides to engage with the book without knowing what change may come, if any, but it does—and he, the world of Fantastica, *and* his "real-life" world all transform as a result.

Now that these main concepts are laid out from *The Neverending Story*, I'll show, how these same steps work to show different kinds of transformations. In *She Never Told Me About the Ocean* there are four female protagonists: 18-year-old Sage, her mother Marella, a medicine woman named Ilya, and the ferrywoman in the Underworld, Charon. Each share their stories of transformation, all of which are inter-related and inter-connected yet are completely different. In each case the character actively seeks transformation. Sage wants to heal "an inherited fear" of "the deep" and find out who she is, independent of her parents, Ilya seeks to share her knowledge before her ultimate transformation of death, Marella seeks healing from the son who died before Sage was born, and Charon wants to leave her boat in the Underworld for a time and transform into a human at least for a while (and does) (McKetta 92).

The portal in this novel is an underwater cave off the coast of Dragon Island that leads to the Underworld and the afterlife. The portal is a cave that the protagonist(s) actively seek. All of the characters grapple with a loss, be it the loss of a loved one, or a personal loss and all of them have a strong sense of striving. To simplify for the sake of example, I'll look at one part of Ilya's story. Ilya goes into the Underworld to retrieve her dead father so she can save her mother from her grief. While she succeeds, her mother isn't even home when she brings back her father's ghost. Was her journey then in vain? Or is this a failed transformation? No, because what really happened by going into the portal and returning is that she gained self-knowledge. Ilya's transformation is both physical (she has white hair when she returns) and an inner transformation of "lessons learned." And, like her white hair, it's a transformation that she will always have with her. Ilya now knows that you cannot save another person from their story or their grief. She passes this inner knowing on to others through her work as a medicine woman and midwife, and to Sage while simultaneously understanding that each person needs to learn this for themselves through their own experience. This example also shows that while Ilya wanted to interact with the portal for a specific reason, the result was something else (and something that was unknown to her before she entered). This "something else" is internalized and then emitted to others through their thoughts, actions, and way of living.

Though the entrance to the Underworld is hidden under the water, it is a place that the people on the island know about and where they release their dead. On one level this novel is the story of birth-death-rebirth—the natural human transformations, so choosing a portal in nature helps anchor the reader to these larger natural cycles while highlighting that the portal is living out its true purpose. That it is a part of the land also means that knowledge of the portal is shared by many people across time, and Ilya says she "learned from somebody who learned from somebody else that in the rocks underneath a certain point of ocean, there is an entrance to the Underworld" (McKetta 35). This is true to the purpose of the portal in the story: it is public, has always been there, will be there for so long as the rocks don't wash away which means that multiple people know about it. This gives the reader clues to expect that multiple characters can and will seek transformation.

Contrary to Bastian's more passive stumbling upon the book in *The Neverending Story*, the characters in *She Never Told Me About the Ocean* actively initiate their own transformation process. The characters find out about this portal through word of mouth and books. The knowledge is available, and it is up to them to decide what they will do with it. When we put this all together, and as a writer considers the nature of the portal itself to be akin to what happens in the story, it helps to see that if the character seeks the portal in a story (and if it's a place in nature—hidden in plain sight but known to have special powers) then this indicates that they are actively seeking inner transformation even if they aren't sure what it will be. The nature of the underwater cave also gives a clue that the character transformations may be hidden but ultimately are not secret and each of the characters share their influence and transformations upon one another and their community.

It feels important to note that a portal doesn't need to be physical, nor does it need to transport a character from their real world to another one. This underscores that it really depends on what kind of transformation the character undergoes to choose a portal that is "on purpose". A good example of this is the egg in "Bluebeard's Egg" by Margaret Atwood. In her re-telling of the Bluebeard legend, Atwood's protagonist Sally is preparing a dinner party for her husband's colleagues, their wives, and her best friend, Marylynn. While getting ready, Sally is preoccupied with multiple anxieties regarding herself and her marriage. As Ed's third wife, she worries that she is a false bride, and he may be cheating on her. Sally recounts her experience taking night courses which she admits, she "may have begun taking the courses in the belief that this would make her more interesting to Ed, but she soon gave up on that idea: she appears to be neither more nor less interesting to Ed now than she was before" (Atwood 143). It's in these night courses that the portal finds Sally in the form of an egg that is an element of a retelling of Bluebeard that her teacher shares with the class.

Sally points to her own obliviousness and nature in relation to the egg when she says, "but how can there be a story from the egg's point of view, if the egg is so closed and unaware" (Atwood 159)? An egg, even an imagined one, is filled with potential of a new life—that does not yet have its own awareness and is not yet realized. She directly engages with the egg as portal for the rest of the story right up until the last lines: "Sally thinks: the egg is alive, and one day it will hatch. But what will come out of it" (Atwood 166)? Sally ultimately does not transform but leaves the reader with a hint that transformation is possible in the future.

This example of how a portal is chosen on purpose illustrates that when the portal is an intangible artefact and is several layers removed from the character (in this case an element within a homework assignment from an oral story) then they might secretly desire transformation but are not yet ready to actively make it happen. These layers of distance from the portal show the layers of distance the character has from their own inner world. The portal in this case is put upon Sally as it was assigned to her—she did not seek it and did not find it by accident. Sally even has "trouble" with this part of the class (Atwood 155). This example also shows that when writing a story of failed or partial transformation, the character doesn't enter a portal to go to another world, but remains in a closed environment with something that is intangible or not real put into their world for them to make decisions about.

~ 4 ~

THERE NEEDS TO BE A KEY
TO THE PORTAL

In addition to how important it is for a portal's nature and purpose to align with the nature of the story being told, there needs to be a way to show the reader what opens, unlocks, or gives the access to the portal and what happens when it is activated. The best way to show this is with examples from each of these three texts.

In *The Neverending Story*, after being prompted repeatedly throughout his reading of the book that only a human child can save Fantastica by giving the Childlike Empress a name (this is the key to opening the portal), Ende shows what happens when the key is used:

> "Bastian was unaware of the tears that were running down his cheeks. Close to fainting, he suddenly cried out: 'Moon Child, I'm coming.'
>
> In that moment several things happened at once.
>
> The shell of the great egg was dashed to pieces by some overwhelming power. A rumbling of thun-

der was heard. And then the storm wind came roaring from afar.

It blew from the pages of the book that Bastian was holding on his knee, and the pages began to flutter wildly. Bastian felt the wind in his hair and face. He could scarcely breathe." (Ende 199)

Once Bastian speaks the name, the portal opens and the worlds merge. Ende shows this merging of external worlds in several ways. First that it is happening "at once" which brings time of both worlds together and into a present place of urgency. Then he moves to something tangible: in Fantastica the great egg is "dashed to pieces," and as a storm wind comes in "from afar," that very same wind comes physically out of the pages of the book and Bastian feels it.

The choice of typography in this excerpt is important as the italics and roman font replace what were red and green text in the original German and English clothbound editions which exactly match the description of the book Bastian is reading in the story itself (Rutherford, 7). In the black and white edition, the story in Bastian's world is in italics and the world of Fantastica are in roman. This stylistic choice gives further clues as to which world and story a reader is in, and as the portal activates, the worlds merge temporarily so that Bastian can enter. As this happens the lines of italic and roman fonts alternate in short bursts adding to the suspense and providing a moment of clear understanding to the reader of what is taking place. From this point on, and until Bastian exits Fanastica at the end of the book (page 437) the typeface is all roman which indicates Bastian's successful entry into the Neverending Story and leaves no question that he has, indeed, left one world and entered another. The italics return when he returns home.

In *She Never Told Me About the Ocean*, the key is handed to Sage (and given to the reader) by Ilya. In recounting her own experience of going to the Underworld, Ilya gives Sage direction and shares her knowledge:

> "You swim out from the shore toward the rocks that rise like jagged tulips. And you tread water, looking until you see a mark on the rock in the shape of a boat. A simple boat, like a canoe. [...] When you see that boat, you've found the entrance, and what you need to do is hold your breath and go under the rock. [...] But that's just the first part. Next you need to get onto that floor of black rock, or else you'll be stuck inside the cave but outside the Underworld—a wet dark limbo. You cannot imagine, Girl, how dark it is under those rocks, cut off from the sun. You must feel around above you for the tiny entrance and hoist yourself up into it. My books said that a full-grown man, with broad shoulders, could not fit through." (McKetta 93-94)

While Ilya's knowledge is the key, the specific instructions give multiple steps—like a ring of keys. Further, not only does someone need to be a good swimmer, a "full-grown man with broad shoulders" would not be able to complete the journey to the Underworld, which excludes those characters in the novel (Sage's father and Lance) yet leaves the portal accessible to the others and tells the reader who to focus on.

When crafting your own key to the portal in your story, it's important to consider not just what it is, and why it's relevant, but to also give an appropriate way for the reader to understand how it operates. In this case the choice of second-person narration stresses the "how" and Ilya provides specific, direct, instructions (the key) for what anyone will need to do to get to the Underworld. The information is direct and unquestionable, and even includes the reader as someone who now has the keys. In using the words "You swim," "You tread," "When you see," "Next you need to," "You cannot imagine," "You must," Ilya sets herself up as an authority, a reliable narrator, and a trusted adult for Sage to look up to all while giving her specific step-by-step instructions of what to do. In doing this she also points out that it is a place for more than one journey; more than one transformation and initiates Sage into the lineage of those who know. She now has the keys to take with her for herself and to share with others. This also illustrates that the kind of key is not just what opens the portal, but reinforces the kind of character transformation(s) a reader can expect. In this story, many inter-related transformations occur (and perhaps even the reader's inner world will be transformed).

Bastian needs to use his voice to open Fantastica, and to transform into someone who can speak his truth whereas Ilya hands the keys of direct experience to Sage. Ilya cannot go on the journey of transformation on behalf of anyone else, but she can offer guidance for others to have the experience for themselves and to grow in their own ways. Sage transforms her inherited fears by learning how to swim, for example. She also transforms into a mid-wife from the start of the story to the end (thanks to Ilya's mentorship), learns that she cannot save her mother, and grows from a teenage child into a woman in terms of her maturity and knowledge.

Sage does not directly touch the Underworld until the end of the story. After she releases Ilya's body into its watery grave she "started to row back but then changed [her] course" (McKetta 243). She "finds the place easily" and she states that "it felt autonomic, like some place I had to go" (McKetta 244). Sage has the keys to the portal, uses them, and even sees Ilya's face as that of Charon, the ferrywoman. She, however, has a yet another kind of exit from the Underworld than Ilya described, as she is pulled back up by her boyfriend, Pupuka. Her exit from the same portal many others have entered is unique and, just as her own story and personal transformation is tied to the others, this exit reminds the reader that Sage was never alone in her transformation. From the beginning, her internal transformation came from incorporating the lessons of others who have gone to the Underworld before her. As she is pulled back up to the surface of the water and is also warned by Ilya-as-ferrywoman to "go back—now," Sage's current phase of transformation is complete and she does not need to fully access to the Underworld at this time (McKetta 245). She can choose to go there one day and will go there in her death (arguably the ultimate transformation). Another way to think about this is a key begets another key. Sage gets to stay aboveground (for now) to work with and be what has already transformed within her and to be the source of information (the key) for others. This is something to consider not just for the kind of story you want to tell, but the integrity of its structure.

The key in "Bluebeard's Egg," is also given verbally but is entirely different to the direct instructions that Ilya gives to Sage in *She Never Told Me About the Ocean* or the words that Sebastian speaks in *The Neverending Story*. In this case the key comes in the form of a homework assignment in Sally's *Forms of Narrative Fiction* class. Another important choice that Atwood made is that this key is provided to the reader not as direct dialogue or voice, but as Sally's memory of her teacher telling the class about the homework assignment. As she recalls the assignment she tells the reader what the key is. Sally recounts that "this time they had to choose a point of view. It could be the point of view of anyone or anything in the story, but they were limited to one only" (Atwood 156). The key then is to "choose a point of view" from a version of Bluebeard that Sally's teacher gives in the oral tradition to the class. The key gives the reader insight to Sally's internal world as she contemplates (and perhaps even struggles) with what to choose.

Sally isn't seeking knowledge of her inner world or transformation, and the key here is foisted upon her by someone else. This is important for her story and potential transformation because even though it is up to Sally to take action and choose something, the assignment is not something she has chosen for herself. This puts her in position to be somewhat passive and somewhat active. The portal itself is what she chooses to write about: an egg. Until Sally starts to think about the egg and what it means, she avoids looking at her internal world, therefore the egg is the place where the internal and external start to meet and there is the potential for Sally to transform. She is reluctant to look inward until something outside of her (a teacher she doesn't particularly like) puts the option to choose something for herself in front of her.

~ 5 ~

THE CONSTRAINT OF RELATIONSHIP IS NECESSARY

Lastly, it's important for a portal to not feel clunky, inserted in the story as a prop for the character only to use it, but an embedded part of the story. In other words, why is the portal necessary? And, if it can just be removed from the story, and the story still makes sense without it, then it's not needed. Like I said at the start, not all stories have portals. From looking at these texts it became evident that the way to do this is to make sure the character is "in conversation" with the portal. I first encountered this idea in an assignment for a course called "Decadence, Degeneration and Decline: The Popular British Novel" taught by Dr. Margaret Deli at Harvard Extension School.

In our final assignment we needed to choose a cultural artefact and put it "in conversation" with one of the books we read in the course to show something we had learned about decadence, degeneration or decline novels. I, somewhat randomly, chose an Instagram post about Loving Kindness (a Buddhist practice) by Jack Kornfield and by putting it "in conversation" with *The Picture of Dorian Gray* argued that when all instances of loving kindness in a novel are killed off or obliterated it is a decline narrative. This is called a lens essay, as you see something new because of looking through the lens of something else. What struck me was the fact that those two items (the novel and the Instagram post) had no relationship whatsoever prior to me not only putting them beside one another but having them "talk to" one another which led me to a new understanding about the text. This application of a portal being "in conversation" with a character (and vice versa) is also what makes one inextricable from the other in a story. It's the glue that binds the two together.

If it helps, you can think of the portal as a character in its own right. The protagonist and the portal are equals: they are both required to tell the story, and both need to be developed and believable. The portal, however, is not seeking to make decisions, work through a situation, or grow. To me, this means the portal is an artefact (or place in nature) that is selected on purpose, has a key to access it, and, from a writing perspective, is a constraint. Working with a constraint is what makes it useful to a writer.

I was introduced to writing with constraints through the Writhing Society at the Brooklyn Public Library. This society was a group of people who met regularly for years, and they followed the principles set out by the Oulipo in

Paris, France. Oulipo is short for Ouvrioir de Littérature Potentielle (Workshop for Potential Literature) and this group of people work with the principle "restrictions can enhance artistic expression rather than stifle it" (Dziak). The Oulipo have many kinds of writing exercises with constraints. One example of a constraint is a lipogram is where you write a story (or entire novel) without a certain letter. Another example I really like is from Katie Kohn's "Advanced Fiction: Writing Fairy Tales" class called three ingredients where you choose three objects and include them all in a story. This exercise has led me to write stories that I know could only have ever existed simply because of the challenge set by incorporating three potentially unassociated items into one story. By working within a constraint, the brain (and your creativity) is more likely to make connections that are new or surprising. Often this means discovering ideas, associations, or having a character make a decision that you may not have considered if the constraint was not in place.

In the case of portals and these three works, the constraint would be to write a story that includes the ingredients portal x and character(s) y: a magical book and a boy or a cave to the underworld and four women or an egg in a fairy tale and an anxious wife. No matter what, the story absolutely must include these ingredients. That's where the relationship or having them be "in conversation" with each other comes in. The constraint can be made to be a bit more complex by saying imagine what happens when you put these ingredients (x + y) together and add in a condition z: they have no choice but to get along. Then what?

This is where you as a writer gets to be open to play, curiosity, and trust. To trust that your character is in charge of their own narrative and, since you have chosen a portal that is on purpose, the next step is to let the relationship unfold naturally. How the relationship between the two unfolds does not need to be figured out at the start—and in fact, it is best to leave this open to your own curiosity as a writer by asking the question: what if? What if a boy who is bullied were to find a magical book in a shop? What if there were several women who sought transformation and they could go to another world? What if an insecure wife was given a homework assignment in her class? Asking the question and having curiosity as you write means that not only will you be surprised as to where your character and the portal go together, but that their relationship is what drives the story. Their relationship will show you where to go, what needs to be uncovered (of which you may not even be aware) and will then also mean that what you write includes both the character and the portal in such an intimately embedded way that it cannot feel forced or like the portal is wedged into the story by force. Yes, it's essential to choose a portal that is there "on purpose" and that is not enough—the relationship dynamic between the portal and character(s) is what makes the portal feel integrated into the story.

The constraint of a relationship between character and portal is what does the work of showing the story of internal development. In each of these works there are too many interactions between characters and their portals to provide examples of all the ways in which they are "in conversation" with one another. The constraint of relationship between the two is consistent throughout a story, and should be. As there are so many, I'll choose one example to highlight what I mean by this. It's from *The Neverending Story* when, after Bastian has returned to his world, Ende clearly spells out that the relationship between Bastian and the book is complete. Ende writes:

> *"He looked for the book he had stolen that day, the book that had started him on his adventure. He was determined to bring it back to that grumpy Mr Coreander. What did he care if Mr Coreander punished him for stealing it, or reported him to the police? A person who had ridden on the back of the Many-Colored Death didn't scare so easily. But the book wasn't there."* (438)

Since Bastian's inner transformation has occurred, the portal is no longer needed and the relationship between the physical artefact and Bastian is over. He is no longer a scared little boy, but someone who can face up to what he has done. His transformed Self no longer needs the book, so it's gone. Yet, as we talked about at the beginning of this paper, human transformation is never complete—after someone learns, grows, and transforms, there is more work to be done. When Bastian returns to the bookshop to confess, he learns that Mr Coreander has also been to Fantastica many times and he tells Bastian that *"there are many doors to Fantastica [...]. There are other such magic books. A lot of people read them without noticing. It all depends on who gets his hands on such books"* (Ende 444). Since the reader in this case is also holding a copy of *The Neverending Story* in their hands this invites them to notice their own relationship with the book and the effect it has had on them.

~ 6 ~

FINAL THOUGHTS

There is a lot to consider when writing a piece of fiction that includes a portal. The craft decisions of what kind of portal to choose "on purpose," how it operates, and what activates it, help show what kind of transformation the character will achieve (or fail to achieve). The question remains: why should a writer place a portal in their work? Especially when a portal isn't required to tell a story or show a character's transformation. There's something to the mystery of consciousness and how the inner world of any human works that is amplified by including an artefact (or place in nature) purely because the portal, its potential, and its magic is unknown to the reader and character alike. Further, if the portal is a place where the unconscious and conscious of a character meet, then it is a powerful tool that, by virtue of it being "in conversation" with a character is a way for the writer to easily show their inner thoughts.

Including a portal means that the character interacts with it throughout the entire story. A portal then is a way to tease out the inner thoughts and dialogue that show growth from the moment the character and the portal meet. The portal is constant but how the character behaves and what they say about themselves and/or how they interact with the portal changes as the story progresses. To choose to have a portal in your story also means you have an anchor to return to over and over in new ways, and as the character transforms, their relationship with the portal drives the narrative forward. This anchor is also something for the reader to have as a point of orientation so that they can track the transformation. Every time the portal and character "touch" in their relationship it's also a touchpoint for the reader.

~ 7 ~

ACKNOWLEDGMENTS

A huge thank you to Deanna McFadden for her friendship and unwavering support of all my writing and publishing projects. She is also the person who led me to the Master of Creative Writing and Literature program at Harvard University's Extension School. It was a year into the pandemic and the school had (unbeknownst to us at the time) expanded their online courses—we signed up. In our very first course together on Zoom, we met the incredible Elisabeth Sharp McKetta and I thank her for being such a warm, caring, smart teacher, for her ongoing friendship, and for continuing to share her work with the world. I ended up taking several classes with Dr. McKetta and they have shaped me as a writer. I also want to thank Dr. Talaya Delaney who was my guide for writing this essay. Right from the start of the thesis, she helped me hone my many, many, many abstract ideas into something concrete. It's a remarkable feat to have taken the thought experiments that felt interesting but overly challenging and have them all come together in this essay. I could not have done this without Talaya. I'm also grateful to my partner, Jim, for being a constant sounding board and pillar of support through this process and for taking me to see an art installation exhibition by Laura Owens at the Matthew Marks gallery in Chelsea, Manhattan which was an immersive (and inspiring) experience of portals.

WORKS CITED

Atwood, Margaret. *Bluebeard's Egg.* McClelland and Stewart, 1983.

Auden, W. H. "The Quest Hero." Texas Quarterly, vol. 4, no. 4, 1961, p. 81.

Burroway, Janet. *Writing Fiction: A Guide to Narrative Craft*, The University of Chicago Press, 2019.

Campbell, Lori M. *Portals of Power: Magical Agency and Transformation in Literary Fantasy.* McFarland & Co., 2010.

Dziak, Mark. Oulipo (Group of authors), EBSCO, 2024. https://www.ebsco.com/research-starters/literature-and-writing/oulipo-group-authors#. Accessed April 30, 2025.

Ende, Michael. *The Neverending Story*, The Penguin Group (USA) Inc., 2005.

Leonie Rutherford. "The Reader in 'The Neverending Story'. -1984 by Michael Ende." *Reading Time (Sydney, N.S.W.)*, vol. 36, no. 4, 1992, pp. 7–12.

McKetta, Elisabeth Sharp. *She Never Told Me About the Ocean*, Paul Dry Books, 2021.

ABOUT THE AUTHOR

Heather Sanderson is a multi-talented writer with a focus on the healing arts. Her *Dreaming with the Plants* series has twenty-two titles in print and centers on spiritual and practical plant medicine for modern times. Her first children's book, *The Dog Who Wanted to be a Butterfly,* came out in 2025. She holds a Bachelor of Arts (Honors) in English Language and Literature from Queen's University, a Master of Publishing degree from Simon Fraser University, and is completing a Master of Liberal Arts in the field of Creative Writing and Literature from Harvard University's Extension School. Her academic writing has appeared in *Book Publishing 1.*